Coaches Make the Difference

Denny Smith

Copyright © 2022 Author Denny Smith

All rights reserved.

ISBN: 9798412191676

DEDICATION

I dedicate this book to Dean Tate, my high school basketball coach, who devoted 31 years of his life to our little town of Morton, Minnesota, and always made sure that we had a chance to play ball. He taught us that there's a big place in the world for us small town kids.

To Dr. John Kasper, my baseball coach at St. Cloud State University, who later was my Department Chair when I was on the coaching staff at SCSU. His sense of humor and his love for his players and family were an inspiration to so many. He made baseball fun and made everyone feel like an important part of the team, including his number three catcher.

To Noel Olson, the Head Basketball Coach and Athletic Director at St. Cloud State. I had the honor of serving as Noel's assistant for four years and will always appreciate everything he did for me as a coach and as a person. Noel later served as the Commissioner of the North Central Conference and was most proud of his role in expanding athletic opportunities for women. His most memorable advice was, "Always treat people right."

To Marlow "Red" Severson, my mentor as a student at St. Cloud State. I was his student manager, and in my senior year I was honored to be a student assistant under his direction. Red instilled confidence in his players, was a master motivator, and his excellence as a coach was demonstrated by his nine championships in 11 years as Head Basketball Coach at St. Cloud State.

To all of the players who made my 31 years of wearing a pair of sneakers an exciting ride. Hopefully your athletic careers were fun, exciting, and rewarding and went far beyond the verdict of the scoreboard. Thanks for the memories.

TABLE OF CONTENTS

	Acknowledgments	i
1	There is Another Way	1
2	The Kind of _____ You Become	6
3	How to Carve a Duck	9
4	Emotional Intelligence	13
5	Awareness Precedes Change	17
6	Who Motivates the Motivator	21
7	Aunt Mole	24
8	A Look in the Mirror	26
9	The Attitude Mechanism	29
10	Keep Winning in Perspective	33
11	Be Your Own Best Coach	38

12	Patience	41
13	Solution Consciousness	45
14	Dealing with Upset People	50
15	How Can We Fix This	53
16	DESC Solution Method	55
17	The Power of Self-Talk	58
18	Keeping Your Self-Talk Positive	61
19	The Power of Belief	66
20	Coulda, Shoulda, Woulda	69
21	She Will Not Change Until You Change	72
22	You Could Be Somebody's Dean Tate	74
23	The Beginning	77

ACKNOWLEDGMENTS

My first tip of the hat goes to Timothy Schmidt of Agency 511 in St. Cloud, Minnesota. In addition to guidance as a business consultant, Tim was instrumental in formatting *Coaches Make the Difference,* designing the cover, and offering suggestions on the book's content and style.

My wife, Pat, not only offered a ton of encouragement, but spent hours reading and re-reading excerpts; then adding creativity and support along the way.

I thank Jo Tate, daughter-in-law of my high school coach, Dean Tate, who you will meet in Chapter 22, for proof reading and offering insight and encouragement to the project.

I appreciate the help of Joe Schmit, KSTP Sports Director and a professional speaker and author, for sharing advice and expertise.

And to all of my friends and colleagues who took time to proof the manuscripts and help tweak the content of *Coaches Make the Difference.* Your help is appreciated.

CHAPTER 1
THERE IS ANOTHER WAY

Purpose

A newspaper article on a non-coaching issue once described me as "a former fist-pounding basketball coach with anger issues." Although it was not flattering, it did contain an element of truth. I grew up during the authoritarian era and my coaching idols, the Bobby Knights and Vince Lombardis of the world, won championships, so I concluded that must be the way to do it. There was an "ends justify the means" mentality. If I did some screaming during the week but we won on Friday, everyone would be happy, and it would all be OK. But at my level, was it really OK?

Don't get me wrong, I could give a pep talk with the best of them, I was pretty positive and upbeat most of the time, I did a lot of things right, I had some pretty good years, and I did win a few along the way, but when it came to dealing with problems and unwanted behavior, my authoritarian style and lack of emotional intelligence stood in the way of me being all that I could have been.

There is a line in Frank Sinatra's retirement song, *I Did it My Way*, that sums up my motivation for writing *Coaches Make the Difference*. "Regrets, I've had a few, but then again, too few to mention." My regrets aren't from using the wrong defense, or not calling a time out when I should have, or making the wrong bench coaching decision, or losing the big game. My regret is that too many times my lack of self-control and emotional intelligence made my players' athletic experience less than it could have been.

Coaches Make the Difference is written to encourage coaches to replace the "my way or the highway" mentality with time tested self-coaching tools that foster more patience, more confidence, an ability to solve problems in a calm manner, to use a more controlled and approachable tone of voice, and to have more fun along the way. I am on a mission to convince coaches that there is another way, and that the other way may be more rewarding and a lot more fun.

Don't get me wrong, instilling a desire to win and pushing your athletes to work to be the best that they can be requires intensity. The best coaches temper that intensity with self-control and emotional intelligence, and their athletes know that they are loved and respected. Keep your tirades to a minimum and at all costs, avoid sarcasm and demeaning remarks. Correct the behavior without criticizing the person.

So I begin with a message based on over middle age/under middle age, and you decide what that is. If you are under middle age, don't wait until you're in your sixties to learn this stuff – do it now. Had I mastered this at age 25, my 30 years of wearing a pair of sneakers would have been even more enjoyable than they were, both for me and for my players, and I probably would have won a few more along the way.

If you are over middle age, know that it is never too late to learn. I am at the age where I have more yesterdays than tomorrows, but I have enjoyed more growth in the past two years than ever before in my life, and growth is exciting.

A Lesson Learned

In my thirty plus years as a coach I got to know some good ones. One of the best was Bob Lateral, the sophomore basketball coach at Tech High School in St. Cloud, Minnesota. He said, "In my early days I was a screamer. I broke a lot of clip boards." One day his Athletic Director called him in and said, "Bob, there is another way."

Taking that advice, Bob went to work on his coaching style and became one of the most level-headed coaches I have ever known. His teams were well-coached, well-disciplined, well-organized, well-behaved, and they won. In fact, he won over 75% of his games as the sophomore coach at Tech. He was also the Girls' Softball Coach and won a couple of state championships and did it without breaking clipboards.

The same was true in the classroom. He was mathematically sound and you could hear a pin drop in the room. He achieved the same climate in his lower-level classes with students at risk as he did with his advanced students and did it all without raising his voice.

Do people who seem to always be in control of their emotional responses ever get angry? Of course they do, but they have learned to channel it constructively. Many times, anger can motivate us to get things done or to work for necessary change, so the challenge is not to master anger but to master your response to the anger. Aristotle said it best.

> **"Anyone can get angry – that is easy; but to be angry with the right person, and to the right degree, and at the right time, and for the right purpose, and in the right way – that is not within everyone's power and is not easy."**

The phrase "not within everyone's power" poses a good question. It may not be achievable for everyone, but is it achievable for *YOU?* That can be answered only by you, but I firmly believe that with determination and practice, almost anyone can master the art of self-control.

An important consideration here is that very few components of self-control and emotional intelligence are "one and done," but are ongoing challenges. Stay aware of your awareness, monitor and adjust as needed, guide yourself back on course when necessary, and give yourself a pat on the back for your progress. You can achieve anything you want to achieve, you can win a few more, and you can keep the clipboards intact.

Where does fear fit in?

Let's examine fear from two standpoints. In my early days, I feared that if I weren't tough enough, I would lose control and discipline would go out the window. As modeled by Coach Lateral, that is not the case. You can probably achieve more discipline with a controlled coaching style when your athletes know that they are going to be treated with respect in all situations. This doesn't mean that problems and unwanted behavior are not addressed, but they can be met with a calm tone of voice and in a corrective rather than critical manner. You can set high standards and still create a climate of mutual respect. It's probably easier that way.

The old authoritarian style used fear as a motivator. The "If they cross me up, I'll show them who is in charge." mentality is fear based, which hinders open communications, creates a toxic "you verses me" climate, and zaps motivation.

Let me emphasize again, we are not talking about lowering standards of either performance or behavior. We would do a disservice to our athletes and to ourselves as coaches if we did. Our goal is to strive for excellence in a climate of mutual respect.

We go to coaching clinics to learn as much as we can about x's and o's, to pick up drills to teach fundamentals, and to gain insight on game strategy. You can also strive to learn as much as you can about leadership and coaching style. When you watch a game and observe fundamentals and strategy, also pay attention to the coach's bench demeanor. Decide what you like and don't like, then teach yourself to do more of what you like and less of what you don't like. How you coach is just as important as what you coach, and that will be the essence of your legacy.

How to Use This Book

This is a free country so you can do as you choose but let me suggest some ideas for maximizing the benefits of reading *Coaches Make the Difference*. Good free throw shooters practice shooting free throws every day. As coaches, we know that repetition is the mother of all learning. So it is with your attitudes, your emotions, and your "people skills." You need to hone them every day to stay at the top of your game as a teacher and motivator.

The book is a series of short vignettes that can be digested in just a few minutes. I suggest that you read it once at a leisurely pace, then pick it up almost daily to refresh the ideas and keep personal positivity at the forefront of your thinking. Read a few pages in the morning or just before you go to sleep at night or keep a copy on your desk and pick it up when you have a few minutes to refresh an idea. Open the book at random, read a few pages, and if the message doesn't float your boat, try another page. You could select a topic from the table of contents to see if one of the chapters is pertinent. Do that for a few weeks, set it aside for a while, then come back and repeat the process.

Repeat this for six months to a year and see if you feel the impact of the spaced repetition. If you find yourself thinking about an idea from the book, you know it is starting to work. If you start acting on the ideas, it is really starting to work. If other people notice the change and say, "Whatever you're on, I want some," you have arrived.

We know that positive attitudes get positive results. If we define attitudes as "habits of thought," we can conclude that doing something every day to refresh your positivity should produce some pretty good results. Give it a try and see what happens.

Warranty

This book comes with a warranty. Well sort of. I am confident that practicing these principles will yield amazing results, both on and off the job. I don't claim credit for the knowledge. Like most speakers and trainers, it is my job to gather information and share it with you. I am confident that if you embrace these concepts and put them into play, you will reap substantial benefit.

Here's the kicker: YOU are the one who makes it happen. YOU are the one standing behind the warranty.

CHAPTER 2
THE KIND OF _____ YOU BECOME

The kind of _____ you become is determined by the kind of person you become, and you can fill in the blank with anything you want. The kind of coach you become is determined by the kind of person you become. The kind of neighbor you become is determined by the kind of person you become. For those of you who are parents, the kind of parent you become is determined by the kind of person you become. In fact, that's where I stole the idea. I was reading an article by a parent trainer and he said that many times parents would ask him what kind of parent they were. He would reply, "Don't ask yourself what kind of a parent you are. Ask yourself what kind of a person you are when you are interacting with your kids. If you are a patient person, you will be a patient parent. If you are an understanding person, you will be an understanding parent. If you are a warm and loving person, you will be a warm and loving parent. If you are the kind of person who focuses on solutions rather than problems and one who handles conflict in a calm and controlled manner, then you will be that way as a parent."

Coaches Make the Difference is all about building a better you. And let me interject an important point here. We are not approaching this from a standpoint of lack. You are already good or you wouldn't be where you are. As coaches, we inspire our athletes to strive to get better every day, so let's approach our attitudes, our people skills, and our emotional intelligence in the same way. As one of America's foremost motivational speakers, the late Zig Ziglar used to frame it, "I'm good, but I'm getting better."

If you were to ask me to sum up everything I talk about and write about in one sentence it would be this: YOU make a difference. You make a difference with your athletes, you make a difference in your community; in fact, you make a difference in the world. Perhaps that is best summed up with this little poem.

> **The task, to build a better world, but I asked How?**
> **The world is such a big place, it's so complicated now.**
> **And I so small and helpless, there's nothing I can do.**
> **But God in all his wisdom said, "Just build a better you."**

It's exciting to know that all I have to do to make the world a better place to live is build a better me, and all you have to do to make the world a better place to live is to spend a little time every day making you a better you. The world strives for love and joy and peace and prosperity and all the good things one person at a time, so that makes you pretty important in the scheme of things. It makes you especially important because as a coach, you work with young people at such an important time in their lives.

For those who would like to be motivators, and that's probably all of us, I have some good news and some bad news. The bad news is this. You cannot motivate others. Motivation is a door with the handle on the inside. The good news is this. You can, however, create a climate in which your athletes will become self-motivated. Perhaps that is best illustrated in this paraphrase of a quote from Haim Ginnot, author of *Between Teacher and Child*.

> **"I have come to a frightening conclusion. I am the decisive element. My daily mood creates the climate. My personal approach makes the weather. As a coach, I possess a tremendous power to make an athlete's life miserable or joyous. I can be a tool of torture or an instrument of inspiration. I can humiliate or humor, hurt or heal, and in all situations, it is my response that dictates whether a crisis will be escalated or deescalated and one of my athletes humanized or dehumanized."**

It is frightening but also motivating to know that the climate you create and the culture that permeates your entire organization makes all the difference in the world. If you create a culture that your athletes want to be a part of and conduct practices that they enjoy, you are indeed a great motivator and you will give your kids lessons and memories that will last a lifetime.

There is something special about coaching that is unmatched in a lot of professions: the thrill of victory, the agony of defeat, the adrenaline rush that comes from competition. But when the final gun goes off in your last game and you hang up your whistle for the last time, the things that you will cherish most are the relationships: relationships with your players, your fellow coaches, the parents, the media. These go far beyond the verdict of the scoreboard.

You have chosen a profession that offers so many intrinsic rewards: the comradery with your players and fellow coaches, the fun and laughter you share with others, the highs and lows that come with the roller coaster ride of winning and losing, the excitement of the final minutes of a close game, but most importantly, the impact you have on the lives of the young men and women you mentor and the memories of their time spent with you.

Coach, you really *do* make a difference.

CHAPTER 3
HOW TO CARVE A DUCK

Ok, it's a strange title, but there is a method to our madness. When my father-in-law took up wood carving in his retirement, he carved a little duck that was pretty good. In fact, we still have it. One of his favorite jokes was to ask, "How do you carve a duck?" The answer is simple. Take a block of wood and carve away everything that *doesn't* look like a duck.

"What does that have to do with anything?" you might ask. So many times, when things aren't working in our life, we want to throw everything out and start over, when in reality all we have to do is to eliminate (carve away) one or two little shortcomings, and we're back on track.

If you would like to develop more patience, every time you find yourself thinking or acting impatiently, carve it away and you are left with a calm and patient demeanor. If you would like a kind and understanding tone of voice, every time you catch yourself talking in harsh tones, carve it away and soon your tone of voice is habitually calm and serene. When you find yourself ready to lose your composure on the bench, carve that away and remain under control. When you catch yourself criticizing one of your athletes instead of calmly correcting their mistakes or unwanted behavior, carve that away and you are left with a teachable moment.

Consider this. The perfect duck already exists within the block of wood. The artist skillfully whittles away everything that doesn't resemble a duck and perfection is manifested. So it is with your coaching style. Perfection already exists within you, so like the artist, as you skillfully whittle away the little nuances that prevent you from being all that you can be, perfection will follow. The tools you need to become everything you wish to become already reside within you. *Isn't that a wonderful thought?*

In these short little chapters of *Coaches Make the Difference*, you will be reminded of time-tested ideas that will help you achieve self-mastery and make "personal positivity" a way of life. Like the game of golf, it's simple, but it's not easy. Take a little stick, hit a little ball into a little hole, and if you do that in four strokes you become a championship golfer. What could be simpler than that? But those who have played the game know it's not easy. It is one of the most demanding sports on the planet, requiring hours and hours of practice. It requires getting out of the rough after a bad shot, just like recovering from a tough loss. Golf takes precision, patience, and emotional control beyond the ordinary. It's just like coaching and the game of life in general.

Being patient, taming your tone of voice, staying calm under fire, treating people with respect and dignity even when they may not deserve it is simple, it's just not very easy; but with practice, desire, and self-discipline, it *is* doable.

Your first task is to do a little self-assessment to determine where you are, where you want to go, and what it will take to get there. On the next page, entitled "Carve Your Own Duck" is a listing of personal/professional skills and attributes. Rate yourself on a scale of one to 10, one being low and 10 being high. When you finish, connect the dots to make a line graph. What you see to the left of the line is where you are. What you see to the right of the line is your opportunity for growth.

Carve Your Own Duck

Below is a list of personal/professional skills and attributes. Rate yourself on a scale of one to 10, one being low and 10 being high.

	1	2	3	4	5	6	7	8	9	10
Patience	.	.	.	.	.	.	.	.	.	.
Confidence	.	.	.	.	.	.	.	.	.	.
Self-control	.	.	.	.	.	.	.	.	.	.
Problem solving skills	.	.	.	.	.	.	.	.	.	.
Staying calm under fire	.	.	.	.	.	.	.	.	.	.
Staying positive	.	.	.	.	.	.	.	.	.	.
Emotional intelligence	.	.	.	.	.	.	.	.	.	.
Approachability	.	.	.	.	.	.	.	.	.	.
Tone of voice	.	.	.	.	.	.	.	.	.	.
Listening skills	.	.	.	.	.	.	.	.	.	.
Getting out of judgment	.	.	.	.	.	.	.	.	.	.
Calm bench demeanor	.	.	.	.	.	.	.	.	.	.
_____	.	.	.	.	.	.	.	.	.	.
_____	.	.	.	.	.	.	.	.	.	.

Reflect for a few minutes on the one or two skills you would like to master first; then practice the principles and techniques outlined in the book to achieve mastery. It will take time and persistence and you will go through your ups and downs but keep working at it. You don't have to tell anyone what you are doing. Just be diligent and quietly go about your quest and you will begin to feel the difference. Nowhere is it written that coaching is about long faces and stern looks, so have a little fun along the way.

[Author's Note: We will often refer to "carving a duck" throughout this book. For those who have read our previous book, *Emotional Intelligence 101: How to Carve a Duck,* you will notice some repetition if not out and out duplication in some of the chapters. *Coaches Make the Difference* is an extension of that work but written with a slant towards coaching. So if you have read the previous book, read on. It's like having more than one tackling drill. It presents two ways to learn the same skills.]

CHAPTER 4
EMOTIONAL INTELLIGENCE

In a game against archrival North Carolina in the 90s, Duke was on top of the conference, undefeated, and ranked number one in the nation. They were down by 10 with just a few minutes to play, but they started one of their classic Duke comebacks. You just knew they were going to win. Duke was within one point with just a few seconds left when their center missed a cold, hard lay-up – he absolutely blew the bunny. They flashed the camera on coach Mike Krzyzewski. He didn't react. There went the undefeated season, there went the number one ranking, and there went the conference lead. You know he had to be churning inside, but he showed no frustration. What a great example of "Emotional Intelligence." Coach K, the winningest coach in NCAA history, ended his career in 2022 with 1202 career victories, a Regional Championship, and a record 13th trip to the final four. His bench demeanor was a key ingredient in his players' ability to stay focused and paved the way to their uncanny ability to come from behind to win. Coach K was one of the best.

Another classic example of bench poise was exhibited by Kansas coach Bill Self in the 2022 NCAA men's championship game. The Jayhawks, down 15 points at half-time, staged a record-breaking championship game comeback to win the title. During their less than impressive first half performance, Coach Self was a picture of calm and poise on the bench. His demeanor and emotional control gave his players the chance to hoist the trophy and cut down the nets. The behavior and sportsmanship exhibited by the coaches, players, and fans throughout both the men's and women's tournaments, from both the winners and losers, was phenomenal. Stanford's Tara VanDerveer, now the winningest women's coach in NCAA history with 1157 career victories, was a picture of class throughout her career, win or lose. Her poise and grace in their semi-final loss to Connecticut was a shining example of keeping everything in perspective. Tennis star Billie Jean King gave VanDerveer this tribute. "You taught us how to win both on and off the court." We can all aspire to provide that kind of experience for our student athletes at all levels. It's why we coach. It's why we play the game.

Defining "Emotional Intelligence"

Emotional intelligence isn't an *emotion*; it's a *decision*. Let me repeat that: it's not an *emotion;* it's a *decision*. It's about teaching yourself to think before you act instead of the other way around. When you make a conscious choice to be more patient, more confident, to maintain composure under pressure, or to trade a harsh tone of voice for a calm and more approachable one, you will be on your way to an ever-increasing level of self-mastery that will add so much success, happiness, and peace of mind, both personally and professionally. Let's look at some definitions of this thing we call emotional intelligence:

1. **"The capacity to be aware of, control, and express one's emotions, and to handle interpersonal relationships judiciously and empathetically."**
   This is good but it is a mouthful and pretty academic, so let's simplify it a bit.

2. **"Skill in perceiving, understanding, and managing emotions and feelings."**
   This is more precise and easier to digest, but there is a third that may be even simpler.

3. **"The ability to keep yourself under control, even when you don't want to."**
   In other words, you'd like to punch their lights out, but you manage your behavior and respond in a controlled manner.

The first two are retrieved from the internet and there are literally hundreds available. I'm partial to the third one because it's kind of my own version and easy to understand. The point is this: it doesn't make any difference which definition you subscribe to – just subscribe to something and *use* it. Develop an ongoing strategy for continual growth and mastery, then apply it.

Achieving a high level of emotional intelligence is one of the surest ways to help you achieve success in any endeavor. Your career success, your relationships, your effectiveness on any committee or in any leadership role, and your friendships are all buoyed by your ability to keep yourself under control.

The third definition talks about maintaining control, *even when you don't want to.* This is a simple measure of your desire level. If you're improving and your determination to hold your cool is stronger than your desire to fly off the handle, congratulations – you are making significant progress. Chalk up the victory and realize that the power to keep yourself calm is yours to own. As you continue to practice, it will become your standard operating procedure.

Coaches Make the Difference has a major purpose: to provide you with the tools and inspiration to master the art of self-control.

Practicing Emotional Intelligence

"Practicing" emotional intelligence may sound strange, but as coaches we know that mastery of any skill takes practice, and lots of it. We often hear about a person with good "people skills," which insinuates patience, a calm bench demeanor, problem solving skills, etc. If these are "skills," they can be taught, learned, and honed. Let's apply principles that we use every day in coaching to do so.

I am told that professional golfers start on the putting green, then go to practicing chip shots and eventually work their way to the driving range. Pitchers warm up with some soft tosses before they work on their fastball. Daily practice routines in almost every sport work from the simple to the complex. Good teachers do the same, working from the simple to the complex.

When you find yourself getting upset over little things, recognize it as an opportunity to practice self-control. I am a member of our local Optimist Club, and one tenant of our Optimist Creed is "To be so strong that nothing can disturb your peace of mind." It's easier said than done, but with practice, progress is possible. Look for opportunities to conquer little challenges; then move from the putting green to the driving range.

Let me illustrate. The pandemic of 2020 curtailed our social life, but it did afford my wife, Pat, and me more together time. We started playing a nightly game of 500 Rummy. Initially I dominated the win column, but then things went south. Pat started stomping me and I found myself using a lot of biblical terms, not in a biblical sense, if you know what I mean. Observing the ridiculousness of getting upset over a silly game of cards, I set a personal goal to curtail my frustration and I went to work. I'm doing well if I do say so myself, and the games are a lot more fun, win or lose. Don't get me wrong, I still like winning, but learning to detach from the outcomes reduces stress and increases enjoyment, and knock-on wood, it's working.

Recently I was putting the cover on our pontoon and things were not going according to Hoyle. It was late at night, it was hot, the mosquitoes were thick, and I was getting frustrated. In the past, impatience and a few verbal outbursts would have been routine, but I kept reminding myself "to be so strong that nothing can disturb your peace of mind." It was a chance to practice on something small to prepare for larger challenges. It may sound silly but try to look upon frustration as an opportunity to practice, then talk yourself into staying calm and maintaining self-control. Do this for six months and see how much more patient, positive, and approachable you are, and how peaceful and serene life becomes.

Apply this across the board in your coaching. When you catch yourself getting upset over little things, rise above it, hold your cool, and handle the situation with poise and confidence. Practice, practice, practice.

In a later chapter on self-coaching, we emphasize that a key ingredient in increasing any of these skills is desire, and there is a good way to measure that. Feeling improvement indicates that the desire is there. Falling short more than you should and making excuses sends a message that you need to intensify your commitment. So joyfully and intelligently get to work and see what happens. I think you'll like it.

CHAPTER 5
AWARENESS PRECEDES CHANGE

Don't do it yet but just say to yourself, "I am going to move my arm." Now move your arm. You said, "I am going to move my arm," then you moved your arm. Here is a profound and powerful question. Who is the "I" and who is the "My?"

We have located the command center in the brain, the part that sends the message from the brain to the muscle, but we have never located the commander of the command center. That is your higher self, your higher awareness, your oneness with the Universe, your "observer," or whatever you want to call it. But regardless of how you label it, it is what makes us different from other forms of life and gives us power as human beings. We have the power to think about what we think about, and how we choose to use that power has a profound effect on everything we do.

The key ingredient in directing that power is awareness. *Awareness Precedes Change,* so be aware of your awareness; and I did say *Be Aware of Your Awareness.* Become your own observer. Monitor (observe) what you are thinking and what you are doing, realize you have the ultimate choice to control or not control your behavior, then choose how you are going to handle any given situation. The late Dr. Wayne Dyer, one of my favorite speakers and authors, says that "You are a sum total of the choices that you make." That bears repeating, "You are a sum total of the choices that you make." Exercising that power of choice can lead to mastery of patience, kindness, happiness, personal effectiveness in dealing with people, using an approachable tone of voice, or any other emotional trait you wish to master. So let's examine four steps to increasing awareness.

Step 1: Unconscious Incompetence
You don't know something, but you don't know that you don't know it. (Or you have a "blind spot." You don't see it as a weakness.)

Step 2: Conscious Incompetence
You're not very good at something, but you know that you are not very good.

Step 3: Conscious Competence
You are starting to master a skill, but you have to think about it every step of the way.

Step 4: Unconscious Competence
You do something so well it becomes automatic.

You learned to walk using these four steps. When you were a baby, you couldn't walk but you didn't know you didn't know how to walk, which was level #1, Unconscious Incompetence. Then you noticed people around you walking, but you couldn't walk yet, which was level #2, Conscious Incompetence. One day you pulled yourself up on the coffee table and took a few steps around the table and everyone thought you were so cute. Then eventually you ventured away from the table and took a few steps on your own, then a few more steps and suddenly you were walking. You had advanced to level #3, Conscious Competence. You were walking but you had to think about it every step of the way. Most people walk down the street without being aware of the mechanics of walking because they have reached level #4, Unconscious Competence. It's automatic.

There is another important point to consider. Step 1, Unconscious Incompetence, could be a possible "blind spot" – something you don't see as a shortcoming. In my younger days, I didn't see my aggressive coaching style as a weakness because my role models were that way and they won championships, so it seemed like the way to go. It wasn't until I recognized that it was a deterrent, both as a coach and as a person, that I was ready to move on to Step 2.

A few years ago I had knee replacement surgery and during a therapy session the therapist informed me I was walking with a limp. I didn't believe her at first, but she convinced me that I was indeed shuffling along so she re-taught me the mechanics of walking. Lift your leg, straighten your knee, come down on your heel, then shift your weight forward. I had to create a new awareness and consciously think about the mechanics (step 3) until it again became automatic. This highlights an important point. As we develop emotional skills, we constantly vacillate between levels three and four.

Let me illustrate. In my previous mind frame, I was not always cordial when dealing with customer service people on the phone. If the shipment was late or there was a mistake on the credit card bill, I had the attitude that I was the customer, so you better take care of me, and you better take care of me right now. My tone of voice was terrible and my behavior bordered on jerkdom. As I raised my consciousness, I realized that the person on the other end was a human being who didn't deserve to be treated that way and that I certainly didn't want to be that kind of a person, so I worked on being more pleasant and cooperative. I monitored my reaction and reminded myself to stay calm and it began to create a different set of behaviors.

One night I was on the phone for about 20 minutes dealing with a problem and as I hung up the phone, my wife said, "You sure were patient." She has not accused me of that very often in our 54 years together, but the fact that it happened is proof that almost anyone can make strides in developing more patience and self-control.

Athletic skills are taught in the same way. My sport was basketball so I will use the example of a right-hander learning to shoot left-handed. Everything starts at steps one and two. As the player begins to learn the techniques of shooting a left-handed lay-up, he or she thinks about it every step of the way until it becomes second nature and he or she masters the skill at the level of "Unconscious Competence." In athletics, we talk about being "in the zone," which is nothing more than a total focus on the desired outcome and letting muscle memory take over. It is, as the gurus describe it, the ability to be "in the moment." Staying in the moment also manifests the best bench coaching decisions.

There are two key ingredients for mastery of any of the skills we will be discussing. The first is awareness, and we will be reminded often that *Awareness Precedes Change*. The second is desire. We talk to our athletes about the importance of having a desire to win. We can apply that same principle to our desire to achieve emotional mastery. Your desire to exercise patience has to be stronger than your willingness to fly off the handle. Your desire to use an appropriate tone of voice has to be stronger than your willingness to scream and holler. In Chapter 10 we will outline four steps of self-coaching, but for now just reflect on this question regarding your desire to improve. "How bad do you want to be good?"

CHAPTER 6
WHO MOTIVATES THE MOTIVATOR?

Motivational speaker Charlie "Tremendous" Jones says that where you are five years from now will be determined by what you read. I was conducting a seminar for a group of elementary teachers and there were signs all over the school about the importance of reading. With all due respect to the x's and o's and teaching fundamentals, inspiring your athletes is not only a key element of success, but the thing that impacts our young people for a lifetime.

So who motivates the motivator? As we mentioned earlier, motivation is a door with the handle on the inside, so keeping yourself positive and in a resourceful state is up to you. The list of tricks for staying positive, even in challenging times, is endless.

If you were to say, "Look, I don't believe in that motivation stuff, but I will try one idea for 30 days, what would you suggest?" It would be this: do something every day to bombard your mind with positive thoughts.

If you enjoy reading, get up in the morning, pour a glass of juice or a cup of coffee and start your day by reading something positive. If you haven't read Zig Ziglar's *See You at the Top,* I highly recommend that you do so. In the mid-80s I read Dr. Gerald Jampolsky's *Love is Letting Go of Fear.* It began to change the way I was dealing with my athletes; it changed my parenting, it changed the way I looked at other human beings, and it improved my outlook on life in general. The ideas expressed planted seeds in my mind that blossomed into powerful and pleasant changes in behavior.

Your body requires nourishment every day. If you feed it a healthy diet and exercise it regularly, you will get healthy results. If you choose unhealthy food and a sedentary lifestyle, you will achieve less than optimum health.

The same is true of your precious mind. Feeding it positive and uplifting ideas yields a whole lot more joy and happiness than wallowing in negativity. You have within you that little thing that is the size of half of a grapefruit that we call the human brain a mechanism that has power beyond our wildest imagination. Take time to nurture and feed that wonderful goal achieving mechanism good stuff every day. Read good books, listen to audio programs during drive time, have lunch with a positive person, make a concerted effort to keep yourself positive and upbeat and you will notice remarkable results.

A friend of mine started a practice of starting his day reading four pages of his favorite book, *The Four Agreements*. He is in his tenth year of the practice and has completed the book over 80 times. I started with my favorite, Deepak Chopra's *The Seven Spiritual Laws of Success*, and it has served as a powerful daily reminder. The impact is minimal at first, but after a few months of the spaced repetition, the ideas are becoming ingrained and are powerful forces in my life. *Coaches Make the Difference* is designed to accommodate the practice of spaced repetition. I encourage you to keep the book handy and read just a few pages often as a constant reminder of the benefits of making personal positivity a way of life and a part of everything you do.

I was asked how I would respond to those who say, "I don't believe in that motivation stuff, I think it's just a bunch of fluff." My answer would be this: "It's fluff until you use it." If you go to a seminar and learn a technique for becoming more controlled and do indeed achieve a higher level of self-control, this "motivation stuff" becomes real. If a workshop helps you deal with your athletes' unwanted behavior in a corrective rather than critical manner, it's not fluff, it's powerful. If you teach yourself to be calm on the bench, this "fluff stuff" produces phenomenal results. We as coaches realize more than a lot of others the impact of inspirational quotes and pep talks. Our locker rooms are usually plastered with them.

Satori

The Zen Buddhist term "satori" means "instant awakening" or "instant enlightenment." What seems to be "instant" may not be instant at all. Liken it to a concept in chemistry. You remember from your high school chemistry classes (of course you do) that an atom has electrons orbiting the outer rings and a nucleus containing protons and neutrons and croutons. You also learned that when an electron revs up enough speed, it jumps to the next ring in what appears to be an instant burst of energy. I have been told that in reality, the electron has been accelerating for a period of time until it gathers enough speed to make the jump. In short, something that appears to be instantaneous isn't instantaneous at all, but a culmination of momentum over time.

That is analogous to your quest for growth. It seems that one day you wake up with self-control or a calm tone of voice and have a "satori," when in actuality you have been making steady progress for a period of time until the consistent effort paid off.

Don't get discouraged or lose sight of your goal when you backslide a little bit. If you take two steps forward and one step back, you are one step ahead of where you were when you began. Do that each month for a year and you are 12 steps ahead of your starting point. Because the change is slow you may not notice it, but it is unfolding in marvelous fashion.

Keep your eyes on the prize and remember that the two basic requirements for success in any endeavor are vision and action. Clearly picture and visualize the behavior and mindset you aspire to, then do what it takes to make it happen. Add determination and a willingness to assume personal responsibility and success is inevitable.

CHAPTER 7
AUNT MOLE

A television commercial depicted a young woman taking her new boyfriend to meet her aunt. Just before she rang the doorbell, she said, "Whatever you do, don't say anything about her mole." When Auntie opened the door, the boyfriend blurted, "Hi Aunt Mole."

Lew Tice, founder of the Pacific Institute, says that you are teleological in nature. Don't let the high falutin term fool you. It simply means that words create pictures in your mind and your creative subconscious leads to fulfillment of those pictures.

What does any of this have to do with coaching? With fifteen seconds left in the game, you have a one-point lead, and your opponent has the ball. During the time out you say, "Don't foul. Don't foul. Don't foul." The picture you paint in the mind is equivalent of the young woman telling her boyfriend not to mention her aunt's mole. Instead of focusing on what you don't want them to do, describe the behavior you want. "Move your feet, keep your hands to yourself, be ready to help out," paints a different picture than "Don't foul." Saying "Don't pick up your dribble," sends a different message than "Keep your dribble alive until the forward is open."

When correcting mistakes, teach for the desired outcome. Former UCLA basketball coach John Wooden, one of the best in the business, would sandwich pointing out a mistake between describing the correction. "We need to get the ball to the other side of the floor. You threw the ball back into the strength of the defense. Reverse the ball."

Words have power beyond belief. The words you choose when talking to your athletes *and to yourself* make a ton of difference.

We will explore the power of self-talk and visualization more deeply in Chapters 18 and 19, but for now, remember that as you convey your instructions to your players, don't say anything about Auntie's mole.

CHAPTER 8
A LOOK IN THE MIRROR

    As I was writing *Emotional Intelligence 101: How to Carve a Duck*, I saw a story on national news that is so relevant to coaching that it warrants inclusion in *Coaches Make the Difference*. In fact, the contents of this book many times parallels the *How to Carve a Duck* theme, which brings up an idea worth reflection. Self-mastery of attitudes, emotional intelligence, and people skills carry over into family life, your career, your relationships, your community involvement, and all other phases of your life, summarized nicely by the "Build a Better You" poem in Chapter 2.

    A youth soccer referee got fed up with the behavior of parents. They were more than just yelling at the referees -- they stormed the fields, violently attacking the refs, opposing parents, and even the kids. They were throwing punches, kicking each other, and shouting obscenities. It was absolutely abhorrent.

    Many of the incidents were caught on video so one ref went on a campaign to spread the videos on social media. Although he may have been partially motivated to embarrass them, his major intent was to let them see themselves in action and do a little examination of conscience. It began to work. As the parents observed the ridiculousness of their less than fourth grade behavior, they began to change.

    One mother wrote to the referee to let him know that she had gone four weeks without yelling at an official, an illustration of the power of the carve a duck process. When she saw herself engaged in behavior that she *didn't* like, she carved it away and was left with a more civil and sportsmanlike approach to her child's youth soccer experience. Carve away the stuff that you *don't* like, and you are left with the perfect duck.

Here's a similar illustration. Television has been instrumental in changing coaches' sideline demeanor, especially at the college and professional levels. In the old authoritarian days, coaches would lose their tempers and vehemently berate their players during the game. But television caught them up close and personal and let the whole world see them in action. It also provided a mirror for the coaches, and I am guessing that their initial thought may have been that they didn't want people see them behave like that, then they moved to the next level. They decided *they* didn't want to see *themselves* behaving that way, so they disciplined themselves to change. Carving away the displays of anger left them with a calm and collected bench and sideline coaching style which probably led to more success and a more enjoyable experience for their players.

You can apply this to any skill. Repeating our previous illustrations, if you want to be more patient, when you catch yourself getting upset on the bench or sidelines, carve it away and keep yourself under control. When you observe a harsh tone of voice, get out of attack mode, settle down, and become calm and approachable. Keep this in perspective. As coaches, we need to push our athletes and drive them hard. We need to be tough, but we can be tough without being demeaning and we can skillfully correct behavior without attacking the person.

Let's revisit our golf analogy that we introduced in Chapter 3. Like golf, self-control is simple but it's not easy. Golfers commit years to mastering the game. It takes hours and hours of practice to hone golf skills and exercise emotional control to be successful. So it is with self-control in coaching. Mastery requires a strong desire, a huge commitment, and a lifetime of practice, but it is achievable.

Self-mastery involves three simple steps which we will discuss in detail in Chapter 11. Observe the way you think and act, decide what you want to change, then change it. Let me remind you that change doesn't happen by Tuesday afternoon. It takes time and persistence, so don't expect perfection, just progress.

One more golf analogy. All golfers make some bad shots and end up in the rough, but the good ones hold their cool, pull the right club out of the bag and work themselves back to the fairway. When you blow it -- and you will -- pull the right club out of your bag and get back on the fairway of life.

Now that we have defined emotional intelligence and the carve a duck principle, let's get on with the business of developing the tools to make all if this stuff a way of life, both on and off the job.

CHAPTER 9
THE ATTITUDE MECHANISM

When I ask my seminar participants "How Important are attitudes?" I invariably get back short answers. "Very." "Critical." "Attitudes are everything." I really believe that most coaches subscribe to the fact that attitudes are an important part of our existence and if that's the case, it may benefit us to take a look at how the attitude mechanism works.

Think -----

Attitudes-----

Behavior-----

Results

The way you *think* determines your attitudes. Attitudes are nothing more than "habits of thought." Your *attitudes* determine your *behavior,* and your behavior determines the *results* that you get out of life. **It all starts with the way you choose to think.**

Let me illustrate. I do a lot of driving in my business and make frequent trips to Minneapolis, which is legally about an hour and a half from my home in St. Cloud. What if coming home from Minneapolis I get into a negative thought pattern about my wife, Pat, and our relationship? "That little tiff we had last night. If she ever brings that up again, I'm going to tell her in no uncertain terms what I think of that. Good gravy, I'm out here beating the streets and she says something like that. If she had done something different five years ago our life sure would be different now."

If I would think like that for an hour and a half, by the time I would get home my attitudes would be pretty lousy, my behavior would be cordial at best, and the results would probably not be very good. What if, on the other hand, I chose to think about the love we've shared for 54 years, or the joy we had in raising our family, or how when I needed her she was right there for me every step of the way. If I would think like that for an hour and a half, by the time I would get home my attitudes would be a whole lot different, my behavior would be a whole lot different, and the results would be a whole lot different and let me ask you this: "What changed?" The only thing that changed was what I chose to think about, but what a dramatic difference in results.

We saw that work over an hour and a half. Multiply that by five, ten, fifteen, or twenty years and you can see that relationships depend on what we choose to think about, coaching style is built on what we choose to think about. To a great extent our lives are determined by what we choose to think about. As Earl Nightingale and so many others have reminded us, "You become what you think about most of the time."

Coaches Make the Difference is designed to serve as a quick reference for keeping yourself resourceful, even during challenging times. The message in Chapter 6 on nourishing your mind is paramount. Start each day by reading something positive. End your day with reflection on positive thoughts, including gratitude. Constantly observe your thoughts and behavior and redirect negativity towards a focus on the good that surrounds you. Taking control of your thinking is perhaps the surest way to take control of your destiny.

When you detect negativity, *carve it away* and allow positive thoughts to abound. There are so many things you can do to keep yourself focused. Read, listen to positive podcasts, take time for quiet meditation, laugh, take a leisurely walk as you marvel at the beauty of nature, exercise, have lunch with a positive coaching colleague and remind yourselves of the importance of maintaining a positive approach to coaching your athletes. When you're in a downer, which we all experience at times, do something to change your mental state and change in behavior will follow naturally. The converse is also true.

Fake It 'til You Make It

When I was teaching at Tech High School in St. Cloud, there were days when I was not filled with the exuberance of human existence, which is a fancy way of saying my backside was touching bottom. As I was walking into school, I reminded myself that I was going to be facing 150 students today, so I had better do something to get into a positive frame of mind. Using the "Fake it 'til you make it" mentality, I changed my frame of mind by changing my activity. I would pick up the pace of my steps, straighten my posture, and pretend to be enthusiastic. I would smile and greet students in the hallway. I would stop in to chat with my positive teaching colleagues. My outlook took a turn for the better and soon I didn't have to pretend any longer; my physiology changed my outlook.

It's Not Fluff

In Chapter 6 we talked about the skeptics who thought this motivation stuff was "just a bunch of fluff." In truth, there is an overwhelming amount of scientific evidence to prove the powerful effects of positivity, healthy self esteem, laughter, and other aspects of a positive approach to life. We no longer just *think* positivity has a powerful impact, we *know* it does. If that's the case, it might be of great benefit to observe, monitor, and adjust your thinking as necessary. Maintaining a positive outlook isn't just a state of mind, it's a *decision,* so you might as well decide to be an optimist. Winston Churchill reminded us that nothing else makes much sense.

It all starts with the way you choose to think.

CHAPTER 10
KEEP WINNING IN PERSPECTIVE

George Sheehan, author of *Running and Being* says that "In play, the athlete realizes that he or she is involved in something that is simultaneously ultimately important and utterly insignificant." During the game or meet the primary goal is to compete at the highest level and to play to win, which is why we buy scoreboards. But what matters in the end is the experience. The game takes a few hours but what you teach lasts a lifetime. In Deepak Chopra's *The Seven Spiritual Laws of Success,* he combines the "law of intention and desire" with the "law of detachment," which parallels Sheehan's reflection about competition being ultimately important yet utterly insignificant. We play to win, but when it's over – it's over.

Michael Jordan nicely put things in perspective. I don't remember the year or the opponent, but I do remember his post-game analysis after he missed the winning shot in game six of the NBA playoffs. He said the moment was "cute." "The ball was in the air, you didn't know if the shot was going in or not, I didn't know if the shot was going in or not -- we were all just waiting." The word "cute" illustrated his ability to put this one in the past and focus on the next one. In game seven, he made the winning shot at the buzzer to clinch the NBA championship. He was a fierce competitor, a hard worker, and a great athlete, but perhaps his greatest piece of advice for players and coaches is this: "Just play. Enjoy the game. Have fun."

St. Cloud Cathedral Coach Bob Karn, the winningest coach in Minnesota High School baseball history, spun a humorous twist to one of his basketball teams when, to put it bluntly, they stunk up the gym. In his post-game assessment he said, "There are 600 million Chinese people who don't know and don't even care how terrible you played tonight, but if you ever play this bad again I am going to call every one of them and tell them."

If you want to win more, teach yourself to handle a loss. When I was coaching in Montevideo (MN), we were playing Alexandra, our nemesis that we had not beaten in a number of meetings. We were trailing by ten points midway through the fourth quarter, and this was before the three-point shot. We made a heroic comeback and with five seconds remaining we had given ourselves a chance to win, but a 15-foot jump shot went in and out and we lost by one. On the radio show the next morning I said, "Let's keep this in perspective. Had the shot gone in, we would be praising our kids for not giving up, for making a gallant comeback, and we would be telling them how proud we were of them and their character. The fact that they *didn't* give up, they *did* make a gallant comeback, and they *did* show great character remained true." The message is this: Give it your best effort, enjoy the journey, but detach from the outcome.

Al McGuire, Marquette's Hall of Fame basketball coach in the 60s and 70s said, "The greatest emotion is winning. The second greatest emotion is losing." What an interesting approach to the old cliché, "Success is a journey, not a destiny."

Let me bare my soul here. Many times I had losing in perspective, but too many times after a loss my self-control went south and I made some less than intelligent emotional choices. To put it bluntly, too often I resorted to yelling and screaming. Those choices negated my positivity and prevented me from being all that I could have been. If we were blessed with an "undo" button in the game of life, those episodes would be my first deletions. To echo our theme from Chapter 1, "There is Another Way," and if this book encourages coaches to implement that lesson, its purpose will have been achieved.

One of the most inspiring examples of a coach keeping things in perspective happened in a high school state championship football game in Minnesota. I don't remember the specifics, but I can relay the inspiring story. A controversial call at the end of the game cost his team the championship. In his post-game talk with his obviously dejected players, the coach said, "Guys, above all, I hope we have taught you how to handle situations like this." He exemplified everything that competitive athletics should be about, especially for our young people.

Bob Brink, who passed away in 2021, was the basketball coach at Rocori High School in Cold Spring, Minnesota for 43 years and the second winningest coach in Minnesota high school basketball history. He finished with 936 wins, 22 conference championships, nine Coach of the Year honors, and a state championship. He was inducted into the Minnesota Basketball Coaches Association Hall of Fame and the Minnesota State High School League Hall of Fame. He was a fierce competitor and was not always cordial to referees and opposing coaches during the heat of battle, but when the game was over it was over. He mastered putting winning and losing in perspective. After a tough loss he would tell his players, "Well boys, don't hang your heads too long, the sun's going to come up tomorrow." I am convinced that this approach to losing was a key factor in his ability to win, and I encourage you to make this perspective an integral part of your coaching.

There are a lot of Bob Brink stories, but perhaps one of the most amusing was when a highly respected official was reffing his final game. With ten seconds on the clock, he blew his whistle and called a technical foul on Coach Brink. When Brink asked what that was for, the official replied, "That's for all the ones I didn't give you over the years." Knowing Bob, he was probably in on the joke.

They Didn't Talk About Winning.

Randy Shaver, current news anchor and former sports director of KARE 11 Television, the NBC affiliate in Minnesota, is in his 38th year of producing a show entitled "Prep Sports Extra," which features highlights of high school sports in the state. He and his staff devote mega-hours in preparation and delivery of a sports program that has earned national acclaim and a number of honors, including Randy's induction into the Minnesota Broadcasters Hall of Fame.

After a topsy turvey 2020-21 season with Covid protocols preventing full fan and student participation, Randy kicked off the 2021-22 season featuring interviews with some of the top high school football coaches in Minnesota. They talked about the excitement of playing in front of the fans and what it meant to the athletes to be reunited with their teammates. One of the players interviewed said, "We missed out last year and now we're just going to play for each other."

Dwight Lundeen, the third winningest coach in Minnesota history, starting his 53rd year as Becker High School's Head Coach, said, "It's not about football, it's about community."

In addition to Lundeen, the featured coaches included Mike Grant of Eden Prairie, Brian Vossen of Lakeville North, Lambert Brown of Wayzata, Justin Reese of Fridley, Jason Potts of Edina, Ray Betton of Shakopee, and Ryan Bartlett of White Bear Lake. Their thoughts centered on the excitement of the upcoming season and included comments like: "I get chills just thinking about seeing the crowd as we walk down the hill. You can smell it in the air. The players are out here, the music's going…. When you take something away, you really appreciate it when you get it back."

These highly respected coaches with phenomenal records didn't talk about winning but reflected on what's really important. When you take care of what's important, winning takes care of itself.

Here's a philosophy that can serve as a guide for keeping winning in perspective. "Some nights you're going to be the kicker and some nights you're going to be the kickee. If you can behave with class in those extremes and in all situations in between, all of the time and energy you put into your athletic career will be well worth the effort." The best way to teach it is to model it.

"Some nights you're going to be the kicker and some nights you're going to be the kickee. If you can behave with class in those extremes and in all situations in between, all of the time and energy you put into your athletic career will be worth the effort."

CHAPTER 11
BE YOUR OWN BEST COACH

Socrates once said, "All learning is self-learning." We all need teachers and mentors, but the reality is that you are the ultimate determiner of your thoughts and behavior. If you don't control your thoughts and behavior, your thoughts and behavior will control you, so let's explore four steps to becoming your own best coach.

Desire

An old light bulb joke asks, "How many counselors does it take to change a light bulb?" The answer is, "Only one, but the light bulb has to want to change." It illustrates the cornerstone for success in any endeavor – *desire*. Desire is paramount and perhaps *the* most important element. Your desire to be patient must be stronger than your willingness to fly off the handle. With a strong desire, you can remain calm on the bench, which leads to better decisions. Your desire to use a controlled tone of voice has to be stronger than your desire to be right or to get in that last zinger. Your desire to be confident must supersede your fear of getting out of your comfort zone and taking a risk.

There is a simple way to measure your desire level. Ask yourself if your ability to maintain control in upsetting situations is greater now than it was a year ago? Is controlling your tone of voice easier than it used to be? If you are still holding onto a grudge or wallowing in self-pity, it may indicate that your willingness to cling to the past supersedes your desire for peace and serenity. If you are not making progress in any of these areas, crank up your determination and make a firm commitment to make progress. Mastery will follow.

No Excuses

One of Dr. Wayne Dyer's last books was entitled *Excuses Be Gone*. As he conducted seminars on the topic, he would invite members of the audience to join him on stage for a coaching session. People would share horrendous experiences like abuse, addiction, childhood trauma, etc. Although he was empathetic and compassionate, he did hold their feet to the fire. He acknowledged the hurt and devastation that was caused by their experience, he recognized that others may have caused them great harm, but he did hold them accountable for their own healing. He encouraged them to get the professional help they needed but emphasized that the ultimate responsibility for healing rested with them.

It is easy to carry a grudge and to wallow in anger and self-pity, and you may have every right to do so, but the outcomes of staying in that state of mind are unhappiness or even depression. You may have been wronged, you may have been treated unfairly, other people may have caused you harm, but the responsibility to heal rests with you. This is extremely difficult, but a necessary step to take if you want to achieve peace and serenity.

Tough losses hurt. The bad call is difficult to deal with. Watching the opposing team celebrate as they hold up the trophy that you and your kids worked so hard for and wanted so badly is not easy to swallow, but you are ultimately responsible for your reaction. Hold your head high and handle the disappointment with class and dignity.

The late Eric Butterworth teaches us that there is a reason why you get upset. "You get upset because you are upsettable." You may be thinking, "Don't lay that on me. You heard what that other person said, of course I'm upset," or "The bad call cost us the game. Who wouldn't get upset?" Eric Butterworth wouldn't buy that argument. You may be churning inside, but you have the power to control your reaction in any situation.

That doesn't mean that you won't blow it occasionally or that you won't ever show anger, but as you work diligently to shorten the duration of your outbursts, you will find the list of things that upset you diminishing rapidly and being upset will be replaced with a calm and controlled demeanor. With practice and persistence you will find that you don't get upset very often because you are no longer upsettable.

Monitor and Adjust

We have said it before and you will be reminded many times throughout the book that "Awareness precedes change, so be aware of your awareness." Be your constant observer.

When you feel yourself getting upset or impatient, observe (monitor) what you are thinking and what you are doing, then adjust and coach yourself into a resourceful state. Monitor your tone of voice, your level of anger, and your reaction to it. Observe whether you are in attack mode or in a state of solution consciousness. Muster all of the emotional control that you can and be accountable for your response. Tell yourself, "I can't control the way I feel right now, but I *can* control the way I think and act."

When you blow it, and you occasionally will, forgive yourself and move on. Mentally rehearse how you will handle similar situations in the future. Picture and visualize yourself reacting with patience and poise. Kindly say to yourself, "Hey, that's not like me. I am a patient, loving person, and the next time I will conduct myself in a calm and confident manner. Then visualize it." (We will explore specifics of self-talk in a later chapter.)

Practice, Practice, Practice

This step is illustrated by the old joke about the guy in New York who jumped into a cab with his violin and asked, "How do I get to Carnegie Hall?" The driver answered, "Practice, practice, practice."

Emotional skills are just that – skills. Like any other skills, they require practice. With attention to detail and practice, they can be learned and masered. None of this stuff is easy and mastery doesn't always come quickly, so make your quest for personal growth and self-improvement a life-long endeavor.

Here's a little mental game you can play. The next time someone is getting under your skin, just say to yourself, "Gee thanks. I have been working at being more patient, and you are giving me a wonderful opportunity to practice."

In coaching we teach from the simple to the complex. Practice patience and self-control in the same way. All of this can be taught and learned, but as Socrates reminded us, all learning is self-learning. That leaves mastery pretty much up to you. No excuses.

CHAPTER 12
PATIENCE

Patience is not an emotion; it's a decision.

Former UCLA basketball coach John Wooden, one of the best in the history of the game, told his then assistant, Denny Crum, "Denny, if you want to be a good coach, you have to learn to be patient." Wooden's advice paid off. After a great career as the Head Basketball Coach at Louisville, Crum was inducted into the College Basketball Hall of Fame.

A woman was stopped at a red light and when the light turned green her car stalled. A guy at the back of the line started blowing his horn and kept on blowing his horn and blowing his horn and blowing his horn. The woman got frustrated, walked back to his window, and said, "Mister, if you would like to go up there and fix my car for me, I would be glad to sit back here and blow your horn for you."

We've all been the guy blowing the horn, some of us more than others. We've all been impatient, some of us more often than others. Patience, like its opposite, is learned and is something anyone can master. There's a lesson to be learned from this story. When things aren't going well in a game or a meet, your athletes don't need you to blow the horn, they need you to help them fix the car.

Thomas Harris wrote a book in the 60s entitled *I'm OK, You're OK* in which he outlined three behavioral responses to emotional situations. Response #1 is that of the child.

I AM GOING TO ACT THE WAY I FEEL

A child gets upset, kicks his or her heels and throws a temper tantrum. The emotions are controlling the behavior. As you know, this is not limited to children. We are all capable of getting upset and letting our emotional state dictate our behavior.

The second response is that of the parent.

<u>YOU</u> ARE GOING TO ACT THE WAY I FEEL

For example, when my kids were growing up they might have asked, "Hey Dad, can we go to the park?" and I might have said, "NO." When they asked, "Why?" I might have answered, "Because I'm in a rotten mood, we can't go." They were expected to behave the way I felt.

This is not limited to parent/child relationships. We've all had our days at work when we warn our co-workers, "I'm in a terrible mood. Just leave me alone."

A teacher had a rock on her desk that said on one side, "Teacher is in a good mood today." The other side informed the students, "Teacher is in a bad mood today." She was telling the kids that they were expected to act the way she felt.

Neither of these responses are necessarily good nor bad, they just are. Anger isn't good nor bad, it just is. Emotions aren't good nor bad, they just are.

There is, however, a third response – that of the adult.

I CAN'T HELP THE WAY I FEEL RIGHT NOW, BUT I CAN CONTROL THE WAY I THINK AND ACT.

This is a beautiful patience affirmation. It's a fancy way of saying. "Count to ten before you do anything."

My wife was putting together a train set for our then four-year-old grandson and things were not going smoothly. She said, "Dylan, I don't know if I can to this." He replied, "Gramma, take a deep breath, clear your mind, and work very, very slowly." She had a high stress job as a clinic administrator and said she couldn't count the number of times at work she would remind herself, "Take a deep breath, clear your mind, and work very, very slowly."

You may wonder where a four-year-old got the idea. He and his father used to wrestle Ninja Warrior style. When they were finished, they would bow to each other, get into a Buddha-style meditative pose, close their eyes, and sit quietly for a minute or two. He experienced the transformative power of patience at age four.

We've all heard the prayer, "Lord, grant me patience – right now." It doesn't happen that quickly, but with practice and resolve, patience *is* possible. You can use the adult response as a tool in a number of ways. In a stressful encounter with another person or when things aren't going well in practice or in a game, silently use the words to calm yourself down, carve away the impatience, and keep your energy focused on your desired outcome. During your quiet time, combine the words with visualization and pre-program calmness into your creative subconscious.

In Chapter 4 we defined emotional intelligence as "The ability to keep yourself under control, even when you don't want to," indicating that patience and emotional intelligence go hand in hand. The key component is desire. When your desire to remain controlled is greater than your willingness to fly off the handle, patience is the natural by-product.

Food For Thought

In Chapter 5 we learned about getting to the level of "Unconscious Competence," which is the level of doing things out of habit, almost automatically. With the consistent practice of reminding yourself that "I can't help the way I feel right now but I can control the way I think and act," patience becomes a way of life and things that used to drive you up the wall no longer upset you. With prolonged practice you discover that, "I *can* control the way I feel," as anger and frustration go by the wayside and serenity becomes a way of life.

I CAN'T HELP THE WAY I FEEL RIGHT NOW, BUT I CAN CONTROL THE WAY I THINK AND ACT.

CHAPTER 13
SOLUTION CONSCIOUSNESS

Murphy's law says that if anything can possibly go wrong, it will, and at the most inopportune time. O'Toole's law goes one step further. O'Toole said, "Murphy is an optimist." Problems exist and present themselves every single day. Period.

When the motivational speakers tout the benefits of positivity we think, "Oh, I get it. All I have to do is turn this little crank in my think machine and my problems go away, right?" That's not the case. You will face challenges every single day of your life, so the goal is not to eliminate problems, but to learn to deal with them in a calm manner and to recognize that it is not the problems that give you the headaches, but your attitude towards your problems that give you the headaches. A speaker friend of mine, the late Mike Patrick used to say, "The problem is not the issue. The issue is how you deal with the problem."

Mike inspired thousands with his story. "In high school, I had the world by the tail. I was a good student, National Honor Society; a good athlete; I was relatively good looking, I got a date every once in a while." But in the first football game of his junior year he went in to make a tackle and the running back's knee pad caught his face mask, jerked his neck, and he was paralyzed from the waist down. He had some use of his hands and arms, but when Mike looked at you from his wheelchair and said, "Folks, the problem is not the issue. The issue is how you deal with the problem," you knew he was coming from the heart.

I can't begin to imagine what he went through. One day the band was playing, the crowd was cheering, there were college scouts in the stands wanting to recruit him; and the next day, in fact for the next 99 days, he was in the hospital in Sioux Falls being flipped upside down every 30 minutes so he wouldn't develop bed sores.

He had a lot of support. His mother was with him every one of those 99 days, the students from his high school in Worthington, Minnesota visited to encourage him, the band played the school song, his father encouraged him to go to college, but Mike knew that overcoming the challenges he was about to face was ultimately up to him.

He relayed an experience about speaking to a group of high school students and after the speech a young girl, down on her luck at the time and not very well groomed, shared her story. Mike encouraged her to have hope, to believe in herself, and to realize that with the right attitude and a lot of determination, she could overcome the obstacles she faced. A few years later he was speaking at a community ollege and a young woman, neatly dressed and oozing with confidence approached him and said, "Do you remember when you spoke at such and such a high school a few years ago?" Mike said, "Yeah, I remember that." She continued, "Do you remember the student that talked to you after the speech, and you gave her a pep talk about believing in herself and changing her thinking?" Mike replied, "Yeah I remember that." She said, "I'm that girl."

Mike's words inspired her to change her thinking and inspired her to believe in herself. His words gave her hope for her future. You can do the same with your players. You can give them encouragement, you can give them hope, and you can help them believe in themselves, regardless of the challenges they face. You can help them understand, by example, that the problem is not the issue. The issue is how you deal with the problem.

Tangled Christmas Tree Lights

You can tell a lot about a person by the way he or she handles three things.

> **A rainy day**
> **Lost luggage**
> **Tangled Christmas tree lights**

One of my former ball players sent me that and the timing was perfect. We were about to take the tree down and my history of untangling the lights was less than pleasant. I would get frustrated and the family knew it was time to back off and leave me alone in my misery. But reflecting on the quote, I decided to stay calm and do the job without getting visibly upset. It took me 15 minutes. In previous years it took the same 15 minutes, so the difference wasn't in the time spent, but in emotional response. The moral of the story is this: Life is a series of tangled Christmas tree lights. Untangle them.

Steps to Solution Consciousness

As the title "Solution Consciousness" suggests, the first step is to direct your mental energies away from the problem and focus on the solution. The second step, clearly identifying the problem at hand is a necessity, but once that is achieved, direct your time and energy towards your desired outcomes. OK Captain Obvious, but how many times do we find ourselves wasting precious emotional energy fretting over the problem instead of using our initiative, creativity, and talent to achieve a successful resolution? Albert Einstein reminds us that we cannot solve problems in the same consciousness that created them.

The third and most challenging is to keep yourself positive and in a resourceful state. Harlan Sanders, better known as the Colonel, had a successful restaurant business but in his 70s the highway was moved seven miles away and his business folded. He took stock of what he could do and decided to sell other people in the restaurant business on the idea of selling his recipes. He became a millionaire and created other millionaires along the way. He achieved his success by helping others achieve their success. From the experience he coined the phrase, "Behind every problem is a bigger and better opportunity if you can only find the solution to the problem." As hard as it may be, muster all of the optimism you can, believe in yourself, tap into your God-given talent and creativity, and keep on keeping on. As you forge ahead, heed Mike Patrick's words. "The problem is not the issue. The issue is how you deal with the problem."

There is so much written suggesting techniques for keeping your head above water as you deal with life's ups and downs. One of my favorites is from Eckhart Tolle's *The Power of Now*. "Resist nothing." Non-resistance moves your energy from a "This shouldn't be happening to me" mentality and points you towards a more productive "How can I skillfully seize the opportunity to learn and grow?" Things are as they are *for now,* so ask yourself what you can do in the moment to successfully deal with the situation at hand. More importantly, how can you teach your athletes to do the same?"

Immediately letting go of mistakes and focusing on the present is a cornerstone of Dr. Cindra Kamphoff's book *Beyond Grit.* She was the director of Sports and Exercise Psychology at Minnesota State University, Mankato, and has worked with college, professional, and Olympic athletes, including Minnesota Vikings wide receiver Adam Thielen. Thielen was almost cut as a freshman but persevered and went on to brilliance in the NFL.

She tells of the story of him fumbling the ball early in the game that led to a Saints score. On the sidelines he made a hand motion which she described as "flushing the toilet," a philosophy he learned at Mankato. The play was over, so there was nothing he could do but get it out of his mind and prepare for the next play. In the waning minutes of the game, he made a brilliant touchdown catch to seal the win for the Vikings.

We see countless examples of great athletes making huge mistakes, erasing them from their minds, and making heroic comebacks to win. The same is true when they play a horrible game but come back to win the next one. They have an uncanny ability to keep their focus in the moment. They may have a certain amount of inherent psyche, but to a great extent, it can be taught and coached. The best way to teach it is to model it.

Take Advantage of the Teachable Moments

Perhaps the greatest educational opportunity offered by participation in competitive athletics is that of teaching kids how to constructively deal with failure and adversity. The word "constructive" connotes "building." From challenges and adversity, athletes learn to build character, class, poise, and so many other attributes that will help them live successful and happy lives. Upon reflection, winning and losing pales in comparison to the fact that as a coach, you are blessed with so many wonderful teaching moments – moments that will endure long after the final buzzer. We've said it before, and we'll say it again. "Coach, you really *do* make a difference."

The problem is not the issue. The issue is how you deal with the problem.

CHAPTER 14
DEALING WITH UPSET PEOPLE

In coaching, and in all walks of life for that matter, there are three things you can count on.

Water is wet
Rocks are hard
You will have to deal with upset people

I was working with a group of bank supervisors addressing the subject of dealing with upset employees. One participant said, "I kill 'em with kindness." When I asked what he meant by that he answered, "First, I get in step. I say something like, 'I'm really glad you came to see me about this, let's see what we can do to take care of it.'" That's a little different from the old authoritarian approach that would remind the employee of the number of people who would love his or her job, then advise them to not let the door hit their backside on the way out.

"Then I listen," which is a hard thing to do because we're all vaccinated with phonograph needles and we like to talk, talk, talk. But he said, "I just listen." Listening goes beyond planning what you are going to say when it's your turn, it means to truly tune in with empathy to what the other person has to say. St. Francis reminded us to seek not so much to be understood as to understand.

"Thirdly, we solve the problem." Solving the problem doesn't mean you have to say what the other person wants to hear. You have policies to uphold, you have others to think about, you have standards to adhere to, so meeting their expectations is not always possible. If you do a good job in steps one and two, your chances of them accepting your decisions are greatly increased.

One day I preceded my request for a favor from my principal by reminding him that I had volunteered mega hours working on a project for the district, thinking that would assure me of a favorable response. He said, "Quite frankly, I have a lot of teachers who volunteer time, and if I let you do this, I would be obligated to grant the rest of them the same favor." It wasn't what I wanted to hear, but because we had always had open communications, I was willing to accept his decision.

He was a former English teacher and I taught math, so we had a lot of differences on grading philosophy and other issues, but we always had civil exchanges and I give him a lot of credit for his ability to model the three steps. Like any of the skills we touch on, they are transferrable to your kids, your fellow service club members, your coworkers, your neighbors, or anyone else for that matter. With a controlled demeanor, you become the soothing element that turns potential conflict into constructive dialogue.

If this strategy works for a bank supervisor, it might fit just as well into your coaching skill set. In coaching, we constantly deal with upset players, parents, the media — there is always someone with an ax to grind. It's part of the profession. Anyone can fix the blame for the problem. Skilled leaders have a knack for getting people to work together to fix the problem. The major challenge is to practice the art of "getting in step," the part of the process that requires awareness, self-control, and mastery of emotional intelligence. As Mike Patrick reminded us in Chapter 13, "The problem is not the issue. The issue is how you deal with the problem."

Steps for Dealing with Upset People

➤ **Get in Step**

➤ **Listen**

➤ **Solve the Problem**

CHAPTER 15
HOW CAN WE FIX THIS?

My Fair Lady is one of the most delightful musical comedies of all time. It was an honor to be cast in our local GREAT Theatre's production of the play and an even greater delight to learn from a phenomenal director. Her knowledge, enthusiasm, and love of theatre were just the tip of the iceberg. Her ability to teach, to lead, and to motivate was second only to her effectiveness in dealing with problems as they arose. She simply would ask, in her usual calm and upbeat tone of voice, "How can we fix this?" What a skill set, and one that any of us can learn in a heartbeat. You can use "How can we fix this?" at work, you can use it with your athletes, your neighbors, or anyone else for that matter. It can serve as a problem-solving strategy that tempers everything you do with self-control. Start by describing the situation you face, then pose the question, "How can we fix this?" When the situation requires a more serious tone, simply modify your approach by saying, "We need to fix this," or, more assertively, "*You* need to fix this." You can use the same approach to resolve your self-imposed problems. "Hey, I really blew it and I'm sorry. How can we fix this?" or "What can I do to fix this?" The power of this simple approach is magnified by a calm and controlled tone of voice.

Correction vs Criticism

Chapters 13 and 14 help us reinforce the idea that demonstrating personal positivity and emotional intelligence is not Pollyannaish. As a coach, teacher, mentor, parent, or in any role that you play as an adult leader, it is your job to correct things that need correcting and to fix things that need fixing; but all of this can be done in a corrective rather than a critical manner. By definition, criticism attacks the person. Correction deals with the behavior but leaves self-esteem intact.

As coaches, we have to push our athletes to work hard, to develop self-discipline and mental toughness, to be well conditioned, to be skilled fundamentally, and to understand the intricacies of the game they are playing. Your challenge is to create a climate that makes striving for all of this a positive and rewarding experience, even during challenging times.

Some situations require you to be stern, but you can be strong and unwavering without raising your voice. Stay out of attack mode and focus on correcting the behavior without criticizing the person. By saying "We need to fix this," or "*You* need to fix this," without displaying anger, you can address the behavior in no uncertain terms but leave the self-esteem intact.

Utilize the emotional skills demonstrated by the bank supervisor in Chapter 14. Get in step by connecting with the person or people you are dealing with, listen empathetically, then reach understanding about the solution course, keeping in mind that you do not in any way, shape, or form have to lower your personal standards or relax team protocol. Keep your standards and expectations high.

CHAPTER 16
DESC SOLUTION METHOD

This is not going to be the most warm and fuzzy chapter, but it is ultimately important to develop and utilize a method for dealing with conflict.

When asked what the most difficult step is in making a confrontation, most of my seminar participants agree that bringing the conversation to the table is the toughest challenge. Dealing with problems is not high on the list of our favorite things to do, but it is so necessary to get issues resolved before they escalate. Not doing so is unfair to the rest of the team and to yourself. Uncomfortable as it may be, when it's Nike time – just do it.

Having a game plan prepares you and your team for a contest and maximizes your chances for success. Talking about resolving conflicts and solving problems isn't quite as exciting as playing for a championship or beating your archrival, but it is an integral part of any leadership role, including coaching. Like preparing for an athletic contest, having a "game plan" for dealing with a problem maximizes your chances for a successful resolution.

Business leaders who resolve issues with skill and confidence increase teamwork and enhance their bottom line. Coaches who resolve issues with skill and confidence also increase teamwork and enhance their bottom line, which in athletics is the win-loss column.

In Chapter 14 we outlined a three-step approach for dealing with upset people when they come to you with a problem. In Chapter 15, "How Can We Fix This?" we introduced a tool for maintaining two critical components of effective leadership that included self-control and an approachable tone of voice. Those proficient in problem solving skills portray seriousness and confront issues in no uncertain terms, but they do so with a solution conscious mindset and realize that mistakes are to be corrected, not condemned.

Four Steps to Conflict Resolution

Describe the Problem
Express Feelings/Results
Specify the Solution
Consequences

When describing the problem, be specific and clearly define the unwanted behavior. "Your attitude in practice is not acceptable. You have been disrespectful to me, you have been ragging on your teammates, you show anger and lack of self-control, and we need to deal with that," or "Your teachers have been telling me your classroom behavior has been out of line, and you need to fix this."

Step two, "Express Feelings/Results" can be as simple as, "This is hurting the team," or "It is dragging your teammates down. They don't deserve to be treated that way."

Step three, "Specify the Solution," has been addressed earlier, but to echo an important point, the solution may or may not be to their liking, but you have an obligation to yourself and to the rest of the team to make sure that your personal and team standards are adhered to.

That leads to step four, "Consequences." In my seminars I have participants put a little wavey line between steps three and four to indicate that consequences can be used sparingly, but they need to be there.

Let me illustrate. A coach I worked with, when addressing a problem with one of his players issued this ultimatum. "If this continues, I will say 'hi' to you in the hallways, I will always show respect, but you will not be able to continue to be on the team." He was stern and the ultimatum was clear but delivered in a calm and controlled manner. He attacked the problem in no uncertain terms without attacking the player's sense of self-worth.

You know and I know that when we get confronted, our first reaction is to get defensive. The same will happen to the person you are confronting, so be willing to cut them a little slack and be defensive – within reason, of course.

DESC is nothing earth shaking. You can find hundreds of conflict resolution models on the internet that provide tools for mentally rehearsing and implementing your strategy. If the problem is complex, you might want to confer with a colleague to have him or her help you develop your game plan. A quick review of Chapter 15, *How Can We Fix This?* might be beneficial.

Confronting problems takes courage and is not always fun, but the benefits are huge. Ignoring them and hoping they will just go away often backfires, so address them with resolve and confidence and do it while they are manageable. Doing so serves the best interest of your athletes, your team, and yourself. You deserve it.

Unresolved problems drain energy and are a deterrent to success, so resolve them, put them in the past, and get on with your mission of creating a culture that your athletes want to be a part of and a climate that makes practice fun and rewarding. Just do it.

CHAPTER 17
THE POWER OF SELF-TALK

A little boy was in the middle of a tantrum at the store and his father said, "Henry, settle down. We're almost done, then we can go home." The boy's behavior continued in the next aisle and the father softly repeated, "Henry, just be patient. We'll be done pretty soon." A third time, the father, in a calming voice, said, "Henry, just a few more minutes, then we're going home." A fellow shopper, so impressed with the father's calm and soothing manner commented, "You were so patient with little Henry." The father replied, "*I'm* Henry. He's *Steve*. I was talking to myself."

When I ask my seminar participants how many of them talk to themselves, most of them raise their hand or nod their head, but not all. At breaktime during one session, a participant said, "When you asked that question, I sat back here thinking, 'This guy is nuts. I don't talk – to – myself.' I suddenly realized that I am always engaged in self-talk."

If you agree that you do indeed talk to yourself, we should address a couple of follow up questions. Do you argue with yourself? If you don't think you do, try this. Stand in front of the mirror some morning and give yourself a little pep talk. Say something like "You are a kind, patient, loving person," and listen to what the voices inside of you have to say. I call them "little twerps," because they are nothing more than that unless you relinquish power to them. My twerps would say something like, "What do mean you are kind and loving? Do you remember when you were a sophomore in high school how you teased Denny Sullivan? You made him feel terrible. And don't tell me you are patient. I heard you screaming at your kids just the other day."

The third question is the most important. Do you win the argument? Whoever wins the argument between you and your twerps determines your attitude, your confidence, your self-esteem, and perhaps even your level of happiness. As simple as it may seem, being the master of your inner dialogue is not always easy, but it is ultimately important and well worth putting time and energy into. What you say after "I am" is critical and an unbelievably powerful force in your life. "I am such an idiot," paints a whole different picture than "I am a kind and caring person." Both, however, do paint a picture.

Your Subconscious Mind

In our wildest imagination we cannot begin to fathom the power of the human mind, but let's take a surface look at its workings. Two major components are the conscious mind, the part of the mind that you think with, and the subconscious mind. The subconscious mind is a goal achieving mechanism that behaves much like a computer. A computer is given information, then responds to that information without judgement. For example, a bank employee programmed the bank's computer to take ten cents out of everyone's checking account and put it into his own. As he did so, the computer made no value judgement. It didn't say "Thou shalt not steal," or "Are you sure you want to do this? You may get caught." It just did what the programmer told it to do.

So it is with your subconscious mind. Every thought, every experience you have had is indelibly etched in the memory bank of your subconscious mind, never to be erased. The time you made the winning free throw in the big game, the time you starred in the high school musical, all of your successes are there. Unfortunately, so are the less pleasant incidents. The time you walked across your neighbor's lawn and got scolded, the time you made a fool of yourself at the school dance, the time you failed your Algebra II test. They are also etched in your memory bank.

If you feed yourself thoughts like, "I'm such a dummy," or "You never do anything right," your subconscious mind doesn't judge, it simply adds the information to its memory bank.

The workings of the human mind are so complicated and complex, and volumes have been written about its power, so one chapter of one book will not scratch the surface of the available knowledge, but let's look at a few simple steps you can take to achieve mastery of your thoughts.

The first step, a theme we have emphasized often, is to create an awareness of what you are thinking and what you are doing. Awareness precedes change. Constantly monitor and adjust your thoughts. When you find yourself wallowing in negativity, carve it away and focus on something positive. Eckhart Tolle, in *The Power of Now,* suggests that when your mind is racing, quiet your inner dialogue by observing things around you: things like the beauty of nature, or noticing a building that you have never noticed before, or marveling at the beautiful blend of colors on a billboard. It quiets the inner dialogue and replaces the negativity with a sense of serenity. Start by telling yourself, "That thought doesn't serve me right now. I am going to focus on the beauty of the world around me," then follow Tolle's advice. Spending time daily in quiet meditation helps you accomplish the same.

You can program your subconscious and enhance your higher awareness with positive self-talk, which is the topic of our next chapter.

CHAPTER 18
KEEPING YOUR SELF-TALK POSITIVE

What do you get when you squeeze an orange? Most people reply, "orange juice," because that's what's inside of the orange. The same is true for us as human beings. When we get squeezed, what comes out is what's inside. If there is a lot of anger, bitterness, and frustration in your subconscious; under pressure, if left unchecked, it will manifest itself in hostile behavior. If, on the other hand, calmness and emotional well-being have been programmed into the subconscious, the resulting response would be much different, at least most of the time.

In review, Lew Tice, founder of the Pacific Institute, says that human beings are teleological in nature, which simply means that your words create pictures in your mind, and your creative subconscious, aided by your imagination, helps move you towards completion of those pictures. Words are powerful. They can humiliate or humor, hurt or heal. They can create happiness and harmony, or they can create anger and bitterness.

Using that as our motivation, let's explore five tips for keeping self-talk positive. We will often use the term "affirmation," which by definition is "a statement asserting the existence or truth of something." Statements like "I am such a dummy" or "I never do anything right," repeated often enough, become "assertions of truth." Statements like "I am a kind and caring person" and "I talk to people in a calm and confident manner," have the same power as their negative counterparts, but produce dramatically different results.

The words that dominate your self-talk manifest in both behavior and emotional stability. Recalling a concept from Chapter 17, your subconscious mind accepts and records your input without judgement, and as we have repeatedly said, "Be careful, because what you say is what you get."

Here are five tips for directing your affirmations towards the positive side of the ledger.

Tips for Writing Affirmations

    A. **First Person – Present Tense.** Use phrases such as "I am" or "I have" or "I enjoy." This indicates that you already have that trait, and your creative subconscious will act accordingly. Phrases such as "I will" or "I am going to" will not elicit automatic response, although they may be a good interim step to start your thoughts moving in a positive direction.

    B. **Be Positive.** Your self-talk must paint pictures of your positive, wanted behavior. A statement such as "I am a patient, loving parent. I talk to my kids in a calm, quiet, confident manner," will send those pictures to your subconscious. A statement such as "I don't want to scream and holler at my kids," will produce pictures of screaming and hollering and open the door to screaming and hollering.

    C. **Do Not Compare Yourself to Others.** You are working to improve YOU. You are trying to become the best possible YOU, not trying to be better than someone else. A key to happy living is striving not to be better than others, but to become better than your former self.

    D. **Be Realistic.** Only affirm that which you can honestly see yourself achieving. If you're not athletically inclined, you are probably not going to make it as a center in the NBA. You could, however, become a calm and successful coach or a great teacher or a respected community leader. Set your goals high but not out of sight. "Go as far as you can see. When you get there, you will be able to see further."

E. **Lock On – Lock Out.** Lock on to your positive thoughts and lock out all conflicting thoughts. The minute you feel doubting self-talk entering your mind, get rid of it and replace it with a reaffirmation of your positive aspirations. The process of positive self-talk will not work if you affirm positively part of the time but let doubting, conflicting, and negative thoughts dominate your thinking the rest of the time. Lock onto the positive and lock out all negatives, regardless of what may appear to be going on around you. Others may determine what *enters* your mind but you, and only you, determine what *stays* there.

Let me illustrate the process by sharing my experience using Lew Tice's advice. Much of my authoritarian coaching style carried over into my parenting, which led to me screaming at my kids more than I wanted to. I had been telling myself, "I don't want to scream at my kids. I don't want to scream at my kids. I don't want to scream at my kids," but the picture I was painting of my behavior was screaming at my kids. In line with Lew's advice, I formulated this affirmation: "I am a patient, loving father. I talk to my kids in a calm, quiet, and loving manner." I wrote the words on a 3x5 notecard, memorized it and repeated it often throughout the day. I would visualize and imagine my kids being upset and me staying calm and under control. Little by little I felt the change.

I started this in the mid-80s, and I would like to tell you that since then I have not once screamed at my kids. If you believe that, there's some ocean front property in Arizona I would like to talk to you about. This leads to review of tip E, "Lock On – Lock Out." When you blow it, rather than give up or make an excuse, take a deep breath, and reaffirm, "Hey, that's not like me. I am a patient, loving person. I talk to people in a calm, quiet and loving manner;" then mentally rehearse handling the situation differently next time.

Whether you use your creative power to affirm achievement of "inside-of-you" goals like patience, confidence, or mastering your tone of voice, or "outside-of-you" goals like a career goal or owning a lake home, it is important to pay attention to tip D, which is to be realistic. To determine whether a goal is realistic or not, determine who wins the argument between you and your "little twerps," those little inside voices. If they convince you that your goal is unachievable, redirect your expectations to something that you can fathom being within reach.

In the 90s, I was having coffee with a friend who said, "I could make $100,000 a year in this business." I asked, "Tom, do you believe that?" He said, "No." When asked if earning $50,000 was believable, he hedged a little. When I asked if he thought he could make $40,000, he didn't hesitate to say, "Yes." I suggested that he affirm that; to picture and visualize himself working hard enough and smart enough to earn $40,000, then moving up from there. Two years later he reached an income level of $100,000. The message is to break your goals into believable, doable chunks, adopt a "go as far as you can see and when you get there you will be able to see further" mentality, then make it happen, one achievable step at a time.

In our next chapter we are going to unite the power of positive self-talk with use of vivid imagination. For now, if the mood moves you, get a 3x5 card or a plain sheet of paper and practice writing affirmations that you can use to assist you in developing clarity, direction, and a sense of purpose. Carry it with you and review it often. Repetition is the mother of all learning.

Here are examples of affirming "inside of you" goals.

"I am a patient, loving person. I talk to people in a kind, soothing, and loving manner."

"I enjoy my self-confidence. I am comfortable meeting new people and making them feel relaxed being around me."

"Good is coming to me from all directions and I am open to receive it."

"I deal with upsetting situations in a calm and confident manner."

"The good I am seeking is now seeking me."

"I accept things as they are for now."

"I have already let go of my anger towards _____."

"Just for today, I will not judge others. I accept people as they are and honor their miraculousness as human beings."

"I let go of the mistakes of the past and press on to even greater achievements of the future." *

"I promise myself that nothing will disturb my peace of mind." *

"I am too large for worry, too noble for anger, too strong for fear, and too happy to permit the presence of trouble." *

*Paraphrased from the "Optimist Creed," Optimist International .com.

CHAPTER 19
THE POWER OF BELIEF

To paraphrase a quote from Will Murray, the leader of the Scottish Himalayan Expedition, "The moment one truly believes and commits, providence moves too, and all sorts of things occur that otherwise would never have occurred." Commitment and belief coupled with vivid imagination are powerful tools that athletes and people in almost all walks of life have used for years to multiply their chances of success. Volumes have been written about the power of visualization in athletics, so it is not our purpose here to explore the process at the doctorate level, but to relate it specifically to you and your coaching style.

Literally hundreds of thoroughly researched studies confirm the belief that affirmations, visualization, and mental imagery increase athletic performance. We don't just *think* this is reality, we *know* it is.

Credit for some of our background information goes to Anees Sehikh and Errol Kurn and their book, *Imaging in Sports and Physical Performance*. Perhaps one of the more significant stories is of Jean-Claude Killy, best known for his achievement of winning a gold medal in three Olympic events. His most significant accomplishment may have been his preparation for a race with only mental imagery. An injury prevented on-snow practice, so he was limited to visualization and mental rehearsal for the event. Killy believes that this race produced one of his best performances, even without the luxury of actual physical preparation.

So many athletes share stories of mental imagery as an integral part of their routine. Former PGA champion Jack Nicklaus said, "I never hit a shot, not even in practice, without having a sharp, in-focus picture of it in my head.... I see the ball going there." Tennis star Chris Evert used visualization in her preparation. She would identify her opponent's strategies, then prepare by visualizing herself countering with her own approach. You can search the internet and find an abundance of studies and stories to validate the claims of the power of visualization not only in athletics, but in business, health care, and almost all areas of human achievement. People who have overcome horrendous obstacles to achieve great heights will attest to the power of optimism and of "keeping their eyes on the prize," which is another way of affirming the power of positive self-talk, visualization, and imagination.

One of my most cherished memories as a coach was when my 1976 Montevideo (MN) basketball team earned me the thrill of coaching in the Minnesota State High School Basketball Tournament. The season started slowly but in January we were starting to play pretty well. One evening my wife, Pat, and I were talking, and I mentioned that we were good enough to get to the state tournament. She said, "You really believe that don't you?" I affirmed that I did, and that the belief was strong. The team had some struggles, even late in the season, but we kept talking about our potential to be a state tournament team, and good things began to transpire. One of our starters got sick before the region tournament and his replacement scored in double figures in both games. We made big plays when we needed to, we made key stops on defense, and everything seemed to unfold in our favor.

As we were walking off the floor at the end of our last practice before the region championship game, I queried one of our players, "Well, Jon, what do you think?" He replied, "Same old story. They'll stick with us for three quarters, but we'll get 'em in the fourth." We had a two-point lead at half-time, then had one of those performances in the second half that come only occasionally and won by 29. To this day I am convinced that the deep-seeded power of belief was a key factor.

When I was an assistant girls' coach at St. Cloud Tech High School, we were a young team and hadn't won too many during the season. Our first tournament game was against our cross-town rival, St. Cloud

Apollo. We used the Will Murray quote about belief to prepare ourselves mentally. In the closing seconds of the game, Apollo attempted a shot that would have won the game. The ball rolled around the rim two or three times then rolled out, sealing our victory. I am not professing that it was providence or some kind of divine intervention, but I do know that belief helped us focus, increased our confidence, and made our preparation for the game fun and exciting.

Not every story has a Cinderella ending, but the power of belief is echoed by almost every winning coach. Believing in yourself and in each other does not guarantee a win, but it greatly increases your chances and creates a more rewarding journey. The power of positive expectancy makes practice more fun for you and your athletes, and that's why we play. So give every ounce of energy you can to being positive and upbeat, give it everything you've got, then quit worrying and detach from the outcomes. Don't give up your intensity or your desire to win, just give up your attachment to the results.

The reality is that only one team is going to win, so keep everything in perspective. To revisit some of the things we talked about in Chapter 10, Marquette Basketball Coach Al McGuire said, "The greatest emotion is winning. The second greatest emotion is losing." Rocori High School Basketball Coach Bob Brink told his players after a tough loss, "Don't hang your heads too long. The sun is going to come up tomorrow." Or the classic example of the coach whose team lost the state championship game on a controversial call by the officials: "Guys, above all, I hope we have taught you how to handle situations like this." He exemplified everything that competitive athletics is all about.

To bring the chapter full circle, let me echo that a few pages of one book will not scratch the surface of something as complex as this, but I invite you to use this process to inspire yourself to exemplify class in all situations. Remember, "Some nights you're going to be the kicker and some nights you're going to be the kickee. If you can behave with class in those extremes and in all situations in between, all of the time and energy you put into your athletic career will be well worth the effort." When you hang up your whistle for the last time and the cheering crowds fade into memory, have them remember *you* as a class act.

CHAPTER 20
COULDA, SHOULDA, WOULDA

Minnesota Vikings fans have had their share of frustration over the years and 2021 was no exception. In their defense, they still fill the stadium, they enjoy tailgating, they loyally cheer their team on during games, and each year they optimistically believe that this is going to be the year we win the super bowl. Like most fans, myself included, we enjoy the privilege of second guessing and giving free advice.

I am a firm believer that you don't go for the two-point conversion until you need to. In a recent game against the Carolina Panthers, the Vikings went for two before they needed to and failed, which altered the course of the game. Unfortunately, my cell phone was in silent mode at the time, so I missed Coach Zimmer's call for advice.

Trailing late in the game, the Panthers mounted a comeback and tied the game with a touchdown and two-point conversion with 42 seconds remaining. The Vikings took the ensuing kick-off and heroically marched into field goal range but missed the winning attempt in the waning seconds. Had they not gone for two before they needed to, the Panther's heroics and the missed field goal would have been moot points.

The Vikings won the overtime coin-toss, marched the length of the field on the opening drive and scored the winning touchdown on a picture-perfect pass from Kirk Cousins to K. J. Osborn.

The point of the story is this: *focus*. As fans, we are free to engage in a "coulda, shoulda, woulda" mentality, but players and coaches don't have that luxury. To give ourselves the greatest opportunity to win, we have to turn our full attention to the situation as it is, not as it could have been or should have been or would have been. You are going to make decisions that don't pan out as intended and players are going to make mistakes, but to waste energy fretting over them is an exercise in futility. So muster all of the emotional intelligence at your disposal and focus on playing the ball where it lies. Had the Vikings allowed themselves to second guess earlier decisions, their focus and their chances of winning would have been diminished.

Recently the Minnesota Gopher Basketball team was trailing highly ranked Michigan State by 20 points with 10 minutes remaining. I was thinking that this is the time it would be so easy to throw in the towel and wondered how they would handle what seemed like a lost cause. Gopher Coach Ben Johnson kept them focused, they kept playing hard and made a miraculous comeback. Had they cashed in on a couple of key three-point shots down the stretch, they would have won the game.

We've all been in contests where winning may no longer be a possibility, so our challenge is to give our athletes something positive to focus on. Getting a hockey team that is trailing by four goals with five minutes remaining to continue to skate hard and stay focused is not an easy task, but having your players achieve that mentality is a gift they will cherish and benefit from for the rest of their lives. Managing to control their frustration and to exhibit class behavior in all situations is a goal that by far overshadows winning and losing. In a recently televised college basketball game with his team losing in the waning seconds, the coach called a time out to remind his players to hold their heads high and to accept the defeat with class and dignity. Not a bad use of a time out.

As hard as it is to do, don't let others get to you. Players at all levels have days when they play horribly. Coaches at all levels make hundreds of decisions, most of them right, but some of them not so right. Others may *suggest*; but you, Coach, are the one who *decides*. It is simultaneously a great privilege and an awesome responsibility.

Former Minnesota Vikings Hall of Fame coach Bud Grant was a master of putting things in perspective. When asked why he made a particular decision that the fans and media didn't like, he responded, "It seemed like the thing to do at the time." If you are to stay focused and be the positive leader your athletes deserve, you can replace the "coulda, shoulda, woulda" mentality with, "It seemed like the thing to do at the time." It brings relief of the self-imposed pressure that we as coaches sometimes inflict on ourselves.

From firsthand experience, I know the devastating effects of self-imposed second-guessing. Even my coaching colleagues advised me to quit beating myself up. It's one of those "coulda, shoulda, woulda" things I am finally conquering in my retirement, which reminds me of the fact that it is never too late to learn. I remind myself often of one of the tenants of the Optimist Creed. "Promise yourself to forget the mistakes of the past and press on to the greater achievements of the future." Just bristle up, grit your teeth, and keep on keeping on.

CHAPTER 21
SHE WILL NOT CHANGE UNTIL YOU CHANGE

Upon completion of a seminar in Worthington, Minnesota, the person who hired me asked if I could give him a ride back to Redwood Falls. It wasn't too far out of my way, so I obliged. Much of our conversation revolved around parenting and he told me of having some problems with their then sophomore daughter. He took her to a counselor and at one point the counselor came out to talk to the father. The counselor said, "She will not change until you change." The father had the typical parental response and replied, "Hold it, Doc. I'm not paying you fifty bucks an hour to tell me to change. You get back in there and change her." The counselor repeated, "I know this isn't what you want to hear, but I am going to tell you again, she will not change until you change."

During my two-hour drive home I had time to reflect, and the reflection was eye opening. At the time, our youngest was dealing with some anger issues and I realized that my authoritarian coaching style that carried over into my parenting was part of the cause, so I went to work on myself. When I changed, he changed. His mother also worked with him, teaching techniques of self-control, which reinforces the idea that these skills can be taught and learned. The impact of that message still resonates as I work to conquer the art and science of self-control.

In chapter two we talked about the fact that motivation is a door with the handle on the inside, so your challenge is to develop a coaching style that creates a climate that allows your athletes to have fun and become self-motivated.

Let me illustrate. I was coaching the sophomore team at Apollo High School in St. Cloud, and this group had not had a history of winning. Early in the season we lost by a big margin to our cross-town rival, St. Cloud Tech, and during our post game meeting I said, "I told you guys to hit the open man, but he should have the same color jersey as you." Unfortunately, that description was not far off base.

After that game, my student assistant and I decided that if these kids had any chance of having a decent season, we had to really crank up the positivity. We were trying to fast break, but they weren't ready for that yet, so we slowed down the pace and simplified everything we were doing. Our major coaching emphasis, however, was to keep ourselves positive and make playing basketball fun. Things started to improve and eventually we were able to speed up our tempo. Reserves started to make clutch plays, we were banking in free throws at critical times, and we went from one and four to nine and 11. The rewards were not just about winning, but the enjoyment the kids and coaches derived from the season.

In our post-season tournament we finished fifth and took home a trophy. The impact of that hit me when one of the players said, "Coach, this is the first trophy we've ever won." I realized that it wasn't about the trophy, but the sense of accomplishment it represented. You don't always have to be the champion to be a winner. Sometimes fifth place feels pretty good.

CHAPTER 22
YOU COULD BE SOMEBODY'S DEAN TATE

I grew up in Morton, Minnesota. I know a lot of speakers and authors claim that they grew up in Morton, Minnesota, but I actually did. In our town of 750 people, my class of 32 graduates was the big one. It is with great humility that I tell you I was All-City in football, basketball, and baseball.

For our centennial celebration in 1987, main street was packed with people. For me, and for many of us, it was a celebration of Dean Tate, my high school basketball coach who you met in the dedication. Dean was an authoritarian from the word go and was not always the most cordial. But in spite of his sometimes "in your face" coaching style, we knew that he cared about us. Known as the "compassionate competitor," Dean devoted 31 years of his life to our little town and dedicated his life to making sure that we had a chance to play ball.

Pat Summitt, the 38-year Head Women's Basketball Coach at the University of Tennessee, upon her retirement, was the winningest coach in NCAA history with a record of 1098-208. She won eight NCAA Championships and 32 Southeastern Conference Championships and played and coached in the Olympics. One of Pat's players described her coaching style this way: "She could be kicking your butt up here and then over here she's hugging you – trying to take care of you. Pat has a great sense of humor, and she had a genuine love for her players." The reason she got by with her sometimes abrasive style was summed up by the phrase, "she had a genuine love for her players."

We are not embracing "in your face" coaching, but sometimes lackluster performance and effort requires you to conduct a practice with a "shake up the troops" approach. You can be tough, however, without being punitive. Here are five things to consider.

1. The best coaches keep their tirades few and far between and avoid being in attack mode.
2. Never, as in never, use sarcasm or demeaning language. It's reverse Nike time – just don't do it.
3. End the tough practice on a high note to rebuild their confidence. "Shake up the troops" practices, used sparingly and skillfully conducted, serve to re-kindle necessary intensity.
4. Return to a "How Can We Fix This?" mentality as soon as possible.
5. Let them know you respect them and care about them. Reflect again on Pat Summit's player's comment, "She had a genuine love for her players."

Getting back to Dean Tate and his passion for making sure we had a chance to play ball. When I was in grade school we didn't have a recreation department but that didn't diminish Coach Tate's determination for us to have a chance to play baseball. He did custodial work at the school during the day, but at 4:00 he came to the ballpark and created a little league program and did so without compensation. He cut sod and created a little league diamond that was later used for our city softball leagues, again on his own time and without compensation.

When I was in college playing town team baseball, we would all meet at the local café after church to enjoy Norma Blank's caramel rolls, coffee, and fellowship. We would look out the window and see Dean Tate lining the baseball diamond so we could play ball in the afternoon. He would tend the concession stand during the game to assist our funding, and never expected nor wanted compensation.

When Dean passed away in 1998, a former teammate of mine and I were walking through the town, down to a population of under 500 by then, acknowledging the fact that there wasn't much left in Morton.

John said, "There wasn't that much here when we were in high school." I answered, "But there was one guy who would never let us believe that." Being from Morton was something he was proud of, and he instilled that pride in us.

Numerous stories surfaced at his wake and funeral. Neil Schmidt talked of a day when, as a fourth grader, he was sitting in the bleachers watching Dean groom the infield. Coach approached him and asked if he was a ball player. Neil answered, "I would like to be, but I don't have a glove." Dean opened the trunk of his car, pulled out an old beat-up glove, and said, "You do now." Years later when Neil was inducted in the Minnesota Amateur Baseball Hall of Fame, upon Neil's request, Dean Tate introduced him. Roger Melquist, a former basketball player and track standout, talked about his family being financially strapped, so Dean bought him a pair of basketball shoes so he could play. So many former players shared similar stories.

After Coach retired, we put together a "Dean Tate Roast," featuring former players, opposing coaches, referees, and fans. Dean knew there was going to be a little gathering but was flabbergasted when he walked into the banquet hall to see more than 200 people in attendance. The speakers relayed funny stories, heartwarming stories, and fascinating reflections of Dean's 31 years as a teacher and coach in Morton, but no one talked about winning. When you take care of the important things, winning takes care of itself.

The purpose of this chapter is to let you know that *you* can be somebody's Dean Tate – that special teacher and coach who really made a difference. In fact, if you have been around the block for few years, you probably already *are* somebody's Dean Tate.

So make a concerted effort to continually tweak your coaching style, make personal and professional growth an ongoing quest, and above all, have some fun along the way. Life is a banquet. Why bring a sandwich?

CHAPTER 23
THE BEGINNING

It may seem strange to close a book with a chapter entitled "The Beginning," but I hope this is exactly that. Don't leave your attitudes, people skills, and personal positivity to chance. Make this is just the beginning of your quest to continually improve yourself as a coach and as a person. Great athletes become great through practice, then they keep practicing to make themselves better, then they practice some more. Tweaking their mental approach to the game is an integral part of what they do. I have yet to hear any of them say they're as good as they can be.

Hopefully you will make *Coaches Make the Difference* just one of many tools in your toolbox to make personal and professional growth a way of life. I encourage you to keep a copy handy – on your desk or near your nightstand or wherever you read – and refer to it often. The book is an easy read that allows you to refresh your **P**ositive **M**ental **A**ttitude in just a few short pages a day. Ideas have impact when you refresh them and put them into practice.

Every day is a new day with new challenges that present new opportunities to test your resilience and your positivity, so prepare yourself daily to answer the call. Yogi Berra reminded us that "90% of the game is mental, the other half is skill." Make sure you get the most out of your 90%.

A Sportsman's Prayer

My first Athletic Director introduced me to Berton Braley's Sportsman's Prayer. Before I close with his words, I want to share a story that is forever etched in my memory that exemplifies the essence of Braley's words.

In Chapter 19 I recounted one of my greatest thrills, the opportunity to coach in the Minnesota State High School Basketball Tournament in 1976. On our way back from the tournament we passed through Prinsburg, the team that we defeated in the region championship game. As we rode through town, the Prinsburg players, students, coaches, and fans lined the highway, cheering as we passed through. What a fantastic display of sportsmanship and what an outstanding demonstration of everything athletics should teach us. I am proud to have been a part of that experience, and I want the people of Prinsburg to know that the legacy they left that day is something they can be proud of for years to come. Braley's poem is dedicated to you.

**In the battle that goes on through life,
I ask but a field that is fair,
A chance that is equal with all in the strife,
The courage to strive and to dare;**

**If I should win, let it be by the code,
With my faith and my honor held high.
And if I should lose, let me stand by the road,
And cheer as the winners go by.**

ABOUT THE AUTHOR

Denny Smith is a former teacher and coach, a speaker, trainer, seminar leader, and author. After 11 years in formal education as a teacher and coach, Denny launched a career as a professional speaker and trainer. During that time he continued to coach from the outside at various levels. A friend convinced him that if he wanted to continue coaching, he should return to the classroom and make education his singleness of purpose.

In 1999, at the tender age of 55, he returned to the classroom as a math teacher and assistant basketball coach at Tech High School in St. Cloud, Minnesota. He retired from teaching in 2010 to relaunch his speaking endeavors with a focus on education.

His sometimes emotional, sometimes humorous, but always sincere approach to his audience and subject matter has been enjoyed in 21 states and Canada.

Made in United States
Orlando, FL
22 March 2023